STICKER PUZZLES

FOR CREATIVE KIDS

Adventures in Treasure Land

Meet
· Ben and Emma ·

Ben and Emma are explorers.
They travel all over the world. This
time, they are in **Treasure Land**,
where mysterious creatures and
precious treasures are hidden.
Let's go treasure hunting while
completing the sticker activity!

Mission

Complete all the treasure activities!
Then put the items on the treasure map.

Emma and Ben wake up bright and early.

Before they start their journey, they share a sweet treat—

a **delicious doughnut**—at a restaurant.

With full bellies, these friends are ready to explore!

▶ Puzzle stickers: page 25. When you finish the puzzle, add the item sticker to the treasure map on page 23. The item sticker is on page 45.

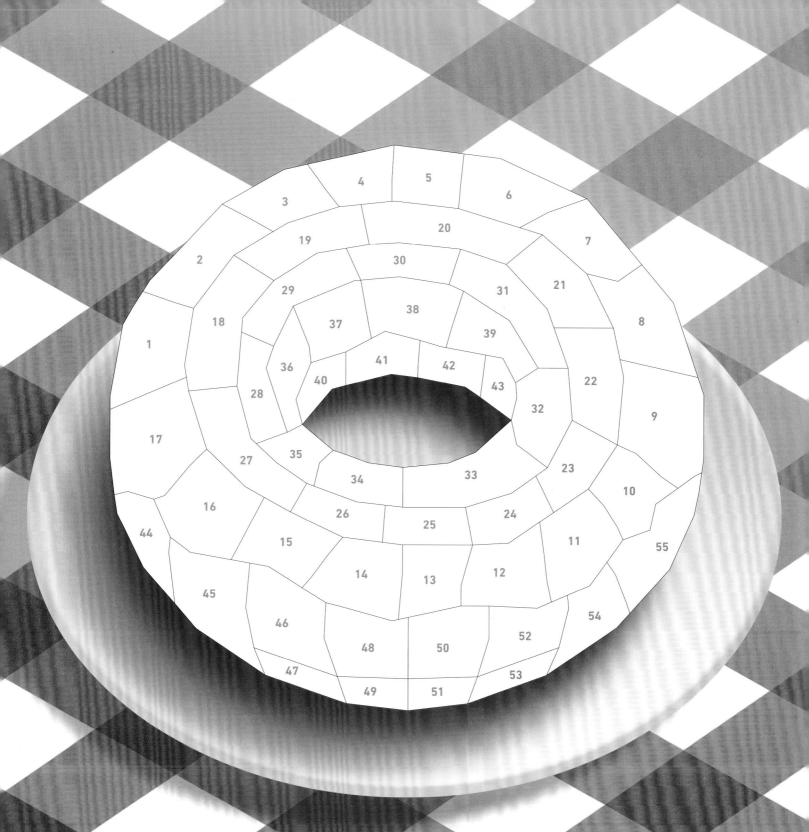

Up, up, and away!

Emma and Ben fly over Treasure Land

in a big, colorful **hot-air balloon**!

As they float away, they wonder

where they will visit next.

▶ Puzzle stickers: page 27. When you finish the puzzle, add the item sticker to the treasure map on page 23. The item sticker is on page 45.

Emma and Ben land in an enchanted garden.

They walk through it and find

a **beautiful flower**. Emma loves the garden,

and even makes a new fairy friend.

▶ Puzzle stickers: page 29. When you finish the puzzle, add the item sticker to the treasure map on page 23. The item sticker is on page 45.

Next stop: the future!

The friends see many modern, high-tech buildings.

Whoosh! A flying car whizzes over them.

Ben hopes to take a ride in it, but there is more to explore.

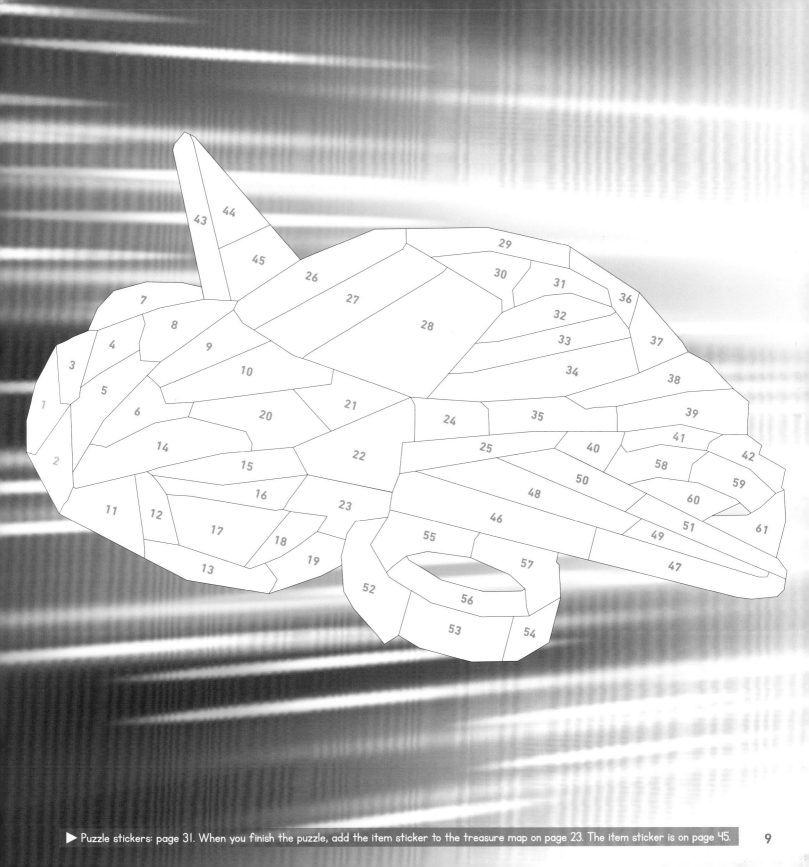

The friends soon find themselves

underwater in a big air bubble!

They glide through the sea and meet amazing

underwater creatures, like this shiny fish.

They wave before continuing on their journey.

Yum!

Emma and Ben were lost in the woods.

But they followed a candy path to a candy cabin!

The friends gather the candy for a snack

before they continue on their adventure.

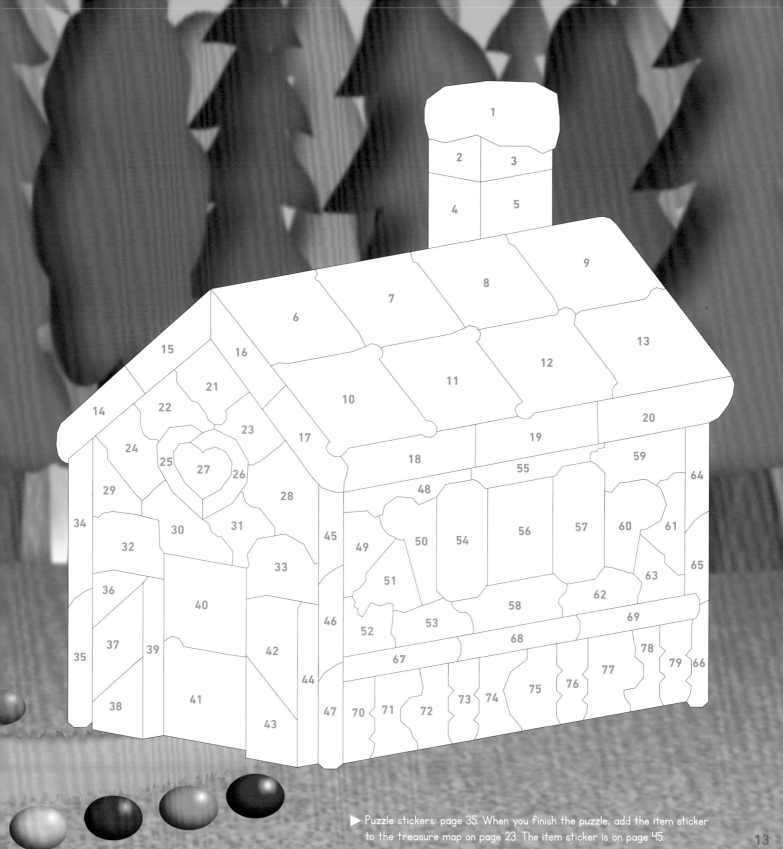

▶ Puzzle stickers: page 35. When you finish the puzzle, add the item sticker to the treasure map on page 23. The item sticker is on page 45.

While exploring the jungle, Emma and Ben discover

a brilliant bird perched on

a branch above them. Emma points to

the extraordinary eggs nestled in the bird's nest.

▶ Puzzle stickers: page 37. When you finish the puzzle, add the item sticker to the treasure map on page 23. The item sticker is on page 45.

Brrr! The friends travel from the hot jungle

to the freezing ice tundra.

They bundle up while exploring this chilly world.

As they put the finishing touches on their snowman,

they wonder who lives in the sparkling ice castle.

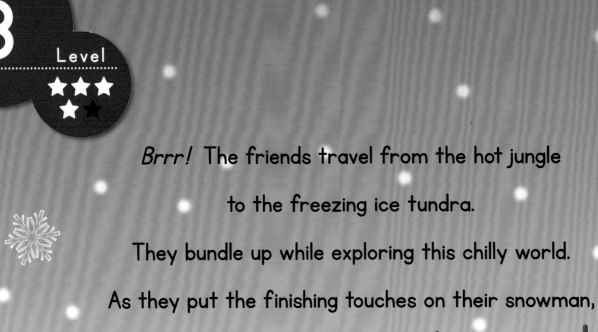

In the desert,

Emma and Ben find an enchanted lamp. When they rub it,

a glittering **star crown** appears

in the night sky. The friends marvel at it,

and then continue on their way.

▶ Puzzle stickers: page 41. When you finish the puzzle, add the item sticker to the treasure map on page 23. The item sticker is on page 45.

18

At the end of their journey,

Emma and Ben encounter a beautiful sight beyond the rainbow.

It's a splendid pegasus

flying over a bright rainbow! They believe

it's the perfect place to end their around-the-world trip.

▶ Puzzle stickers: page 43. When you finish the puzzle, add the item sticker to the treasure map on page 23. The item sticker is on page 45.

Treasure Map

Did you enjoy your trip to Treasure Land?

When you finish the puzzles,

put the things you collected along the way

on the treasure map!

You can find the item stickers on page 45.

Stick them wherever you like!

Magical Adventure Memories

These are the things the friends discovered on their adventure.

① Delicious doughnut

② Hot-air balloon

③ Beautiful flower

④ Flying car

⑤ Shiny fish

⑥ Candy cabin

⑦ Brilliant bird

⑧ Ice castle

⑨ Star crown

⑩ Splendid pegasus

From the supervisor

Children love stickers. This is because sticker play is good for their brains! Recognizing and using patterns to create a picture strengthens spatial recognition circuits, such as the parietal lobe. Peeling and placing stickers develops the somatic sensory area. The fun stories nurture a lively imagination. And solving puzzles encourages curiosity. The future is reflected in the sparkling eyes of children who hold this book in their hands for the first time!

Mogi Kenichiro (*Supervisor · neuroscientist*)

Mogi Kenichiro is a neuroscientist from Tokyo, Japan. He is a senior researcher at Sony Computer Science Laboratories, Inc. and lectures at the University of Tokyo and Japan Women's University.

We did it!

Cover design by Nunotani Chie

Illustrations by NuQ

Supervised by Mogi Kenichiro

For page 3.

25

Stick these wherever you'd like!

For page 15.

42 9 33 12 6 72 20 10 83 11 2 7 40 17 3 1 43 64 44 76 47 29 24 84 8 4 71 69 26 59 31 46 65 38 35 45 56 39 5 68 87 79 18 41 22 51 50 36 55 73 13 28 70 67 52 77 66 15 27 30 81 80 62 32 25 19 21 57 16 54 34 49 60 23 75 85 53 63 14 82 78 48 86 74 61 58

37

For page 17.

39

COLLECTION STICKERS

Place stickers ① to ⑩ on the treasure map.
Put the leftover stickers anywhere you want!